Agnes, the Giant and the Bridge

by Ian MacDonald

illustrated by Irina Mileo

AF584132

Agnes worked on her farm. There were always cows to milk. There were always eggs to fetch from the barn. However, Agnes really wanted to be an engineer.

Lance dreamed of being a farmer. However, any beast made Lance quiver and shake. Even little mice left him trembling.

"I wish I could create a great invention," sighed Agnes.

"I wish I could be brave," sighed Lance.

As Agnes and Lance walked home, they had a shock.

"Oh no, look at the bridge!" gasped Lance. "It's that giant again."

The giant had smashed the bridge. Stones lay scattered. Sticks and logs floated away in the water.

The giant lived in the castle on the hill. He had a wild beard and huge feet. The villagers never knew when he would visit.

Each time he came, he took all the food.
Each time, he stomped back over the bridge.
Each time, he left it smashed and broken.

The farmers needed the bridge. Without it, they could not reach the fields. The birds pecked all the grain. With no grain, there would be no bread to eat.

The villagers worked together to clear the mess. They knew the giant would return.

"We must find a way to stop the giant," said Agnes.

"Yes, but how?" asked Lance.

"I have a plan," said Agnes.

That night, Agnes whispered her plan to Lance. He listened hard. It sounded very technical.

The next morning, Agnes started the preparations. She would make a new bridge! Agnes cut tree trunks and shaped them into wheels.

Agnes worked all night. She was tired and her hands hurt. Now the bridge was complete. Agnes was ready for the next step of her plan.

Lance set off for the castle. He had eggs and apples in a basket.

“I must be brave!” he muttered.

Lance reached the giant's gate and knocked. His hands and legs were trembling with fear. The giant opened the gate angrily. Then he spotted the basket and licked his lips.

"Catch me if you can," yelled Lance.

Then Lance ran! With a loud bellow, the giant lumbered after him.

Lance raced along the dark paths.

He climbed over fallen branches.

He skipped across babbling streams.

The giant was always a little way behind.

At the bridge, Lance raced to the other side. The giant stepped onto the bridge. Lance heard the sound of creaking ropes and clicking cogs.

The bridge began to tilt up into the air. The giant slipped as the bridge rose higher. With a booming yell, he splashed into the water.

The villagers rescued the giant from the water. They talked to him and gave him food.

"I'm so lonely," sniffed the giant.

"I have a plan," said Agnes.

Lance started working on Agnes's farm. The animals didn't seem so frightening now.

Each day, the giant would help Lance on the farm. He didn't feel lonely now.

So what about Agnes? Well, she began to plan her next bridge!

Make And Test A Paper Bridge

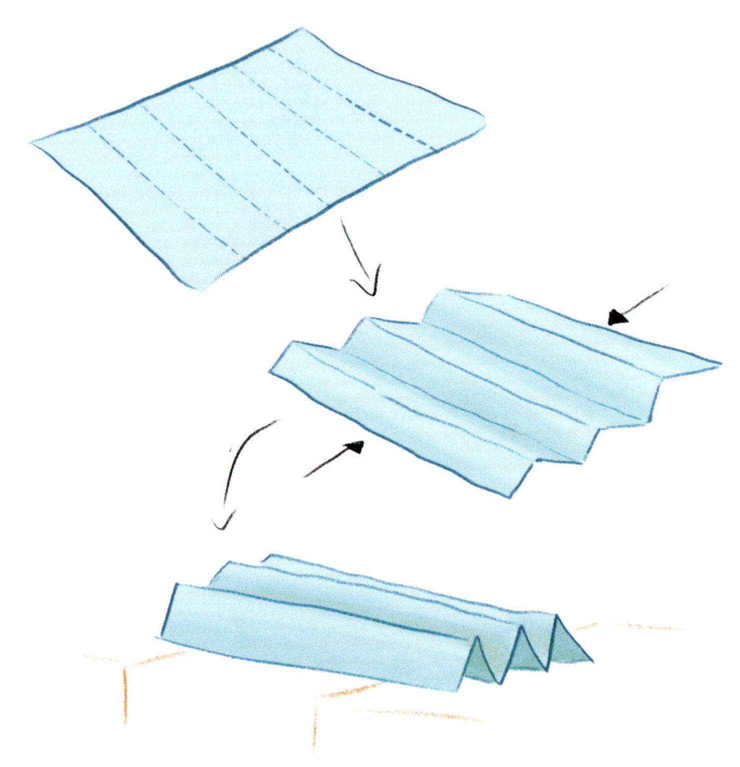

Try folding the paper in different ways.

Can your bridge stretch across two piles of books?

Can you put a weight on your bridge without it collapsing?

Encourage students to link the activity with the events in the story.